THE BOUNCE BACK SERIES

MESSY

By Nicole Powell

Sincere thanks to Graham Williams and the staff at The Lifeflow Meditation Centre.

Cover Illustration Copyright © 2017 by Nattyboo.
Cover design by Nicole Powell, Mar'Yana Kachmar and Pankaj Ranthala.
Illustrations by Nicole Powell, Mar'Yana Kachmar and Hristina Bashevski .
Editing by Kerry Thornton (Chief Editor), John Clancy and Janette Parr.
Thanks to Upwork for providing so much talent.

However, if you think it could be of benefit to someone you know, please share it with them. It was designed to create as much fun, laughter and connection as possible in a world where our children are becoming increasingly disconnected from each other, and their natural environment.

First Printing, 2018.

ISBN 978-0-6481471-6-9

Nattyboo Publishing
PO Box 177
GRANGE, SA, 5022
AUSTRALIA

www.nattyboo.com

PreFace

"We do not inherit the Earth from our Ancestors, we borrow it from our children."

Ancient Indian Proverb.

Messy is the second book in *The Bounce Back Series.* This series was created to empower children and provide them with the strategies they need to overcome adversity and be resilient when facing life's challenges. It encourages children to cultivate a sense of kindness and forgiveness towards themselves and others, and to view mistakes simply as opportunities for learning. In order to achieve these goals, we need self-respect and respect for others. We also need to understand the emotions that drive our lives. Then we can learn to work with these powerful forces rather than hide from them, pretend they don't exist, or be their passive recipients. By encouraging children to understand their emotions and take responsibility for themselves and their choices, they will eventually become the drivers of their own destinies and enjoy an increased sense of confidence, freedom, and empowerment. This gives them the most valuable reward of all: the opportunity to create a life they can love.

The genie in *Messy* represents our combined social conscience. He endeavours to help people understand that their actions have consequences. Consider for a moment that we live on a rock hurtling around the sun at approximately 108,000 km/hr. This rock is the only home that we have in an infinite space, and we share it with countless other life forms. We all need clean water, disease-free land and crops, a complex food web, stable weather patterns and favourable, unpolluted, atmospheric conditions. Yet, how often do you see an adult throw their cigarette butt out a car window or a child drop rubbish on the ground when they think no one is looking? They believe that their actions are isolated and thus, have no consequences. *Messy* is a reminder to us all, to respect the finite reality of our lives and the Earth that underpins it.

The Bounce Back Series was created after the unexpected death of my brother Greg, at age 46, leaving two young children, Max and Amber. The genie resembles Greg and is my attempt to teach the life-lessons that many take for granted; lessons he will never have the opportunity to teach his children. Remember, they are children for such a short time, and they are the recipients of the Earth that we leave them.

FOR MY BROTHER GREG

Max and Amber were playing with some friends they'd just made,
when they noticed two boys eating lunch in the shade.

The children were friendly, and had just moved to town.
So, they smiled, walked across, said "Hello", and sat down.

They ate lunch together and played in the sun,
but no wrappers were placed in the bin. No, not one!

As their last piece of rubbish was thrown on the ground,
a strange box appeared with a thunderclap sound.

It was a dodecahedron that flew all about.
When it finally landed, a genie popped out!

He sat in a spaceship that was white and bright red.
He looked at the children. "Why do that?" he said.

"If you want to live in a huge garbage tip,
just jump in my spaceship; we'll take a short trip."

A trip on a spaceship? Of course they all went!
To a planet called Messy was where they were sent.

In a big pile of rubbish the children were dropped.
On the planet called Messy, the mess never stopped.

The food was all rotting. The whole place smelled bad.
The children of Messy were lazy and sad.

They threw their rubbish all over the place.
The planet was covered with old junk and waste.

It filled up the schoolyard; it hung from the trees.
Wherever they walked, it was up to their knees.

Their garbage had killed every fish in the sea.
There was nothing to eat; those kids were hungry.

The children of Messy had not learned respect.
They were sad, they were sick, and their planet was wrecked.

The genie explained, "Now can you see?
Our actions decide what our future will be.

If all children acted like you did today,
our Earth would be filled with waste and decay.

We have only one home in an infinite space,
so learn to respect and look after the place.

If we pollute the Earth's surface and poison the sea,
the food chain will die, and then so will we!"

The children felt worried, "We just didn't know!
Please send us home, and we'll have one more go.

We don't want to live in a huge garbage tip.
We want to go back and change what we did."

The genie smiled gently. "You've learned some respect.
You now understand that there's cause and effect.

You're young, you're still learning, but now can you see?
What we choose really matters. Don't you agree?"

The children all nodded. "Can we fix it?" they said,
"so the people of Messy are happy and fed?"

"Of course," said the genie. "We choose what we do.
If we make different choices, the results will change too."

So, all of the children and the genie as well,
started cleaning up Messy, improving its smell.

They worked hard together to clean up the place,
and when they were done, they flew off into space.

They returned to their schoolyard and picked up their mess.
The genie was happy, "You've changed. I'm impressed!

If you look after the planet, it will look after you,
and your parents, your children, and their children too."

Suggestions for Parents

Children who have grown up in a healthy environment possess a natural awe for life. That is why a walk to school can take so long. Every puddle has to be jumped in, every leaf examined and every hill rolled down. However, as we grow up so many of us lose this wonder and life can feel like an endless marathon of commitments and obligations.

So, how do we help our children retain the wonder of their childhood and develop high self-esteem? How do we help them feel a deep connection to the Earth, so that we can create a culture in which the environment no longer needs protecting?

In order to help your children achieve these goals, you may find these suggestions useful. But remember:

- They are only suggestions.

- They are aimed at children between 5 and 10 years old, but might work for older or younger children.

- They may not be appropriate for all situations, or all children. You know your children best, and can use them at your own discretion.

- Different approaches have been included because all families are different. Choose those that are in line with your family values and disregard the rest.

The suggestions are in five steps:

Step 1: It starts with you.

Step 2: Where's the respect?

Step 3: Return the awe.

Step 4: Some activities to try with your children.

Step 5: A Sleeping Story.

Step 1: It starts with you.

"Children copy the people around them. So if you want them to be happy, well-adjusted and altruistic you should be that way first."

You might enjoy completing this exercise to check whether or not you are 'living' your values. Children copy what we **do**, *not* what we say. Therefore, it may be beneficial to model sound environmental principles. They don't need to be grand acts. Composting vegetable scraps or creating a worm farm can be great fun and good for the garden at the same time!

Step 1: From the list below, select 5 of the most important things in your life then list them on the following page. Add your own ideas if you wish.

the environment	your health	your children	your family
helping others	money	career	feeling good about yourself
friends	education	happiness	social justice

Step 2: Now prove it.

Record how much time you allocate to each item per week. Be specific about what you do. The exercise it designed to show that what we THINK we are doing can be quite different from what we are ACTUALLY doing. If you cannot find any supporting evidence, from your daily life, that you DO value those things, you can either change what you value or change the time you allocate to it. It can be beneficial to repeat this exercise frequently as a 'life' health check.

What Am I Really Doing With My Time?

	Things I value most	What have I done in the last week that demonstrates that I really value this part of my life?	How much time do I set aside each week for this value?
1	The environment	• Put out the recycling. • Worked on bush care project. • Planted vegetables in my garden.	3 hours
2			
3			
4			
5			

Step 2: Where's the respect?

"Many of us spend our lives searching for miracles, never realising that we are one."

Dr. Graham Williams.

Because children watch and then mimic so much of what we do, it is important to model the kind of behaviour that we are attempting to cultivate in them. Your tone of voice, choice of words and actions all reflect whether you see your children as being worthwhile or an annoyance; astute or inept. It is not enough to tell a child to have respect, you have to show them. Children need to develop respect for themselves, respect for others, respect for our planet and all of the life that inhabits it. A by-product of this type of reflection is heightened self-esteem as your children begin to recognize the staggering enormity of the miracle they are living.

You may enjoy reflecting on these ideas together.

1. We live on a rock hurtling around the sun at approximately 108,000 km/hr. Our solar system orbits The Milky Way Galaxy at around 828,000 km/hr. We are moving at a phenomenal pace through the vast, uncontrolled environment of space. In this context, it seems incredible that we exist at all, and yet how many children ever stop to reflect on this fact? This rock is the only home that we have in an infinite space, and we share it with countless other life forms that we rely on for our survival. We all need clean water, disease-free land and crops, a complex food web, stable weather patterns and favourable, unpolluted, atmospheric conditions. Take some time to explore these facts with your children. Read books, watch documentaries or videos on the internet and discuss what you have learned together. This can become wonderful family time as you discover new things together and children can begin to appreciate the astounding nature of their existence.

2. Then, if they are interested, consider all of the environmental conditions and thousands of chemical reactions that are required for a single flower to blossom and reach maturity. Have them contemplate what is required for a solitary human baby to be born, grow up and reach old age. Then extrapolate that to the countless other species that inhabit the Earth. It is mind blowing! Yet, how many adolescents lament the way their bodies look instead of being astounded by its very existence?

3. We live at a time unprecedented in history. Never before have humans been able to walk into a supermarket and take such a huge range of food straight off the shelves. Until recently, people had to grow or catch their food, and this is still the reality of life in many parts of the world today. Yet, how many of us contemplate this as we load our supermarket carts?

If you are interested in highlighting this point to your children, here are some fun family activities you might enjoy.

Try growing just one family meal in your garden. This will help your children understand how reliant we are on the natural world and the amount of work, and time, involved in obtaining just one meal. This can be an excellent exercise in gratitude and may help them view a trip to the supermarket in a completely new light.

Many apple orchards and strawberry farms allow you to hand pick your own produce. This can be a great family day out as children learn where their food comes from. They will also see how much work is required by others for it to be served on the table.

Take their money boxes with you on a well-planned subsistence camping trip or picnic. Take their fishing rods or their berry collecting buckets, and let them forage for their dinner (or afternoon tea if overnight is too much). Having to collect food is an excellent lesson in respect for a number of reasons:

a) It teaches children how difficult it can be to amass enough food for afternoon tea let alone breakfast and dinner. Even if they do manage to gather enough, it lacks variety.

b) If they fail to gather any food at all, without shops their full money boxes are useless. They soon understand that money is worthless in the natural world. What IS valuable is knowledge, food, water, shelter and each other. Money is simply a trading tool. Once our needs are met, no amount of extra money will make us any happier. This can also help children to understand that we are very reliant on other people for our modern day comforts and survival. It is the work of others that produces food and places it in the supermarkets for our convenience. We each play a very important, but often unnoticed, role in contributing to the well-being of others in our society.

c) Depending on the age of your children, they can also begin to understand that in order to eat and stay alive, almost every organism on the planet, including humans, must consume other life forms. Have them consider the inordinate amount of other life forms such as carrots, potatoes and peas they must eat from birth to death just to stay alive. This can also be a wonderful lesson in appreciation and respect, as children begin to understand that they are part of a process far bigger than themselves.

Step 3: Return the awe.

"Keep close to Nature's heart…and break clear away, once in a while, and climb a mountain or spend a week in the woods. Wash your spirit clean."

John Muir.

As working parents, in modern society, we live incredibly busy lives. Many of us are trying to juggle careers, family commitments, time with friends, sport, education and a myriad of other pressures, many of which are unavoidable. Life can begin to feel like a never-ending marathon of commitments, and our joy and enthusiasm can evaporate.

This endless busyness can result in many of us becoming trapped in our thoughts, worrying about things that have already happened or planning for future events. Without the ability to turn our attention from our thoughts at will, and focus on the sensory input from our bodies, we risk losing our awe for life.

We forget that the only place we can really live is where our bodies are, in the present moment. Young children know this. That is why they are usually unconcerned with time pressures, and when you ask them what they did at school that day, they say, "I can't remember!" For them, the moment has passed and they are on to the new present moment. This is where parents can learn from the wisdom of their children.

If you have a busy life, and find it almost impossible to get any time alone, try 'Pressing Pause' with these quick exercises. They will help shift your focus from your thoughts to your five senses. Notice the brief sense of joy and peace that occurs during these quiet moments, when you reconnect with your body and the environment around you. If you wish, share some of these exercises with your children.

- Take your morning coffee, tea or milk outside. Take a moment to notice how it tastes.
- Pay attention to the sunlight filtering through the leaves of the trees.
- Listen to the sounds around you - the birds, a child laughing, a car driving by.
- Feel the breeze on your face.
- Take a moment to notice any smells in the air.
- Notice how this makes you feel.

DEEPEN THE EXPERIENCE

You can enhance any activity in this way. Next time you take a shower, wash the dishes or eat you lunch, try following these steps in order to enrich the positive feelings in your body and mind.

1. **Before you begin, calm and focus your mind.**

    Do this by taking a long, slow breath in and then breathe out with a deep sigh.

    Allow yourself a moment to step out of your mental chatter, and let your body and mind relax.

2. **Focus your attention on your chosen activity.**

    Do this by scanning SLOWLY through the five senses, noticing one sense experience at a time. Notice how each experience looks, smells, feels, sounds and tastes.

    Give yourself permission to thoroughly enjoy whatever you are doing.

3. **When your mind wanders off into thoughts, GENTLY let go of the thoughts and return your attention to your chosen activity.**

    When your mind wanders, and it will, calmly and gently accept that this has happened and return your attention to one of the five senses.

4. **Notice how you feel when you do this**

    We each have an incredible body. It takes care of countless chemical reactions on its own, fixes itself when it's hurt and reproduces itself. All we have to do is feed it, give it a drink and let it sleep, and it takes care of the rest itself. Yet, many of us spend our days disassociated from our bodies, worrying about things that have passed, that we can do nothing about, or planning for the future. When we recognise this and return to the sensory experience of our body, in the present moment, feelings of dissatisfaction and disconnection vanish and we experience a deep sense of joy and wonder. We have the delightful feeling of coming home.

Step 4: Some activities to try with your children.

"In this modern world where activity is stressed to the point of mania, quietness as a childhood need is too often overlooked."

Margaret Wise Brown.

In order to produce a generation of children who will protect and nurture the environment, they must first have had the opportunity to experience it for themselves. Many adults nostalgically recall childhoods filled with wonderful memories of hours of outdoor play. Yet, Millennium Children may be experiencing a very different reality. The digital-focused age, coupled with shrinking backyards and increasing economic pressures, have resulted in growing numbers of children leading sedentary, indoor lives with digital focused play time. This can be problematic because children's bodies are full of energy and want to move. All that energy is going to go somewhere! If it is not channeled into constructive outdoor play, behaviour problems are highly likely to occur because the basic needs of children's bodies are not being met.

If you want to enjoy some quiet time with your children, where they can slow down and connect with the world around them, you may like to try the following suggestions. Not only are they wonderful opportunities to enjoy the natural environment and find some quiet time, but they also create family memories your children can cherish.

1. Take some buckets, spades and bathers and head to the beach. Pack a drink, a snack and a change of clothes for the children, so you can stay for a while. Enjoy the sounds of the ocean, the breeze on your skin and the feeling of the sand on your bare feet. By leaving the house and going out, you won't be distracted with household chores. Instead, allocate yourself some time to step out of your thoughts and into the sensory experience of your body. Watch your children and learn from them. Young children are very in touch with their bodies so, if you wish, join in their play and share their delight as they enjoy their bodies and their senses.

2. Take a picnic to the park, or find a restaurant with an outdoor setting. Enjoy a glass of wine by yourself, or with your partner, while your children hunt around for the items detailed on their Treasure Hunt list (included). This list is glued to the front of a paper bag and then children fill their bags with the items as they find them. Make sure you instruct them to stay where you can see them, in case they get overenthusiastic and vanish into the shrubbery! If you wish, encourage them to work as a team, collecting the listed items together. Once they have finished, they can show you their treasures and collect their agreed reward. If you want to maximise your quiet time, take some coloured pencils and crayons with you and encourage the children to design and decorate their treasure bags before setting off!

3. Go for a hike and take a break in a peaceful place, where you can hear the sounds of nature. Sit quietly together for a few moments, listening to the sounds, smelling the plants and noticing the colours and textures of the life all around you. If your children are settled, you may be able to take turns sharing what you hear. For example, "I hear a frog croaking. What do you hear?" Allow your attention to expand outwards, letting the sounds come to you, noticing each new sound as it appears in your attention. Notice the silence between each sound. Try the following exercise if you wish.

- PRESS PAUSE by taking a deep breath in and then breathe out with a deep sigh.

- Become aware of all the sounds close to you - the sound of your breathing, the sounds of your children or the rustling of the leaves in the breeze.

- Now listen out as far as you can. Check that you are listening in all directions - in front of you, behind you, to the left and the right.

- You may notice a feeling of expansion as you do this.

- Notice each new sound as it comes to your attention. Do not search for it, but allow it to come into your awareness as you expand your attention outwards.

- When you get distracted by thoughts, become aware of them and then gently return your attention to just listening.

  Notice the sense of peace you experience as you do this.

When your children get bored sitting quietly and listening, they may like to create a natural masterpiece. They can collect anything of interest that they find lying on the ground such as rocks, branches, bark, soil or fallen leaves. Whatever captivates their attention! Then, they allow the ground to be their canvas and create a picture using all the material they have found. You can finish by having an imaginary exhibition and invite their favourite sports stars, singers or actors. (Of course, that would be you!). While they are busy creating their artworks, you can continue enjoying the sounds of nature. If that doesn't work, just resume the hike!

4. Try upcycling! If you live in the centre of a big city, parks and nature trails may be a considerable distance from your home. However, you can still promote environmental awareness by encouraging children to think about what they are putting in the garbage each day. They can create something new and beautiful from empty tissue boxes, soda cans, ice cream sticks, milk cartons or old plastic containers. Empty yoghurt containers can be transformed into beautiful crayon holders or pots for plants. Use them to plant seedlings for a herb garden that your children are responsible for looking after.

5. Many children love to create and adorn things. If you wish, allow them to decorate your recycling bin to engage their interest. If they thrive on competition, hold an art competition and award prizes to the most inspirational messages contained within the art. Alternatively, hold a recycling competition. See who can find the most material lying around the house to recycle or upcycle.

6. Many cities offer monetary incentives for recycling bottles and cans. If you feel it's appropriate, offer this as a method of earning additional pocket money. It's good for your wallet, and good for the planet.

7. Join a community garden in your area. Urban areas frequently set aside small plots of land where interested community members can join together to produce a garden. This can be a wonderful experience for children as they make friends in their local area, and connect with nature at the same time.

8. Have 'wrapper free' days at school when no disposable waste is packed into lunch boxes.

Other suggestions you may enjoy are:

- Find tadpoles in the local creek. Encourage your children to return them to their natural environment before they leave.
- Find some trees in the park to climb.
- Go to a quiet campground, or just camp in your back yard.
- If you don't have a backyard, or the weather is too hot or cold, set the tent up in the lounge room and pretend to camp.
- Stargaze before bed.
- Have a bonfire and roast marshmallows, as you listen to the fire crackle.
- Have a day off from structured activities and just play outside.
- Go for a walk at sunset, find a quiet spot to sit and watch the sun go down together.
- Have a picnic in the park.
- Dance in the rain and then jump in a warm bath together.
- Take a nap outside under a tree.
- Rake up all the autumn leaves and then jump around in them.
- Make cubby houses out of tree branches and leaves and then play games in it.
- Go on a family bike ride.
- Make mud (or snow) pies and serve them for lunch at your pretend café.
- Roll down a grassy hill over and over and over again! Have rolling races to see who can get to the bottom first. Wear long sleeves though. Grass can make you itchy!
- Walk or jog to school.
- Collect rocks for a rock zoo, or visit the real zoo in your area.
- Spend a day at the botanic gardens.
- Encourage children to create a garden bed of their own, and look after it! If you have limited space, plant an interesting indoor garden with the tops of carrots and other vegetable cuttings from the kitchen
- There are a great deal of 'nature play' suggestions on the internet. Have fun trying them out.
- If you live in a big city and your children have limited access to the natural world, you can use *A Questing Game* (included) to stimulate your child's imagination, create positive self-talk and produce feelings of connection and peace. It will also encourage them to go to sleep on time!

Resources

From Me to You

"The Earth was small, light blue, and so touchingly alone"

Alexey Leonov.

I hope you enjoyed reading *Messy* as much as I enjoyed writing it! The way we behave is seldom changed just by reading words. We need consistent reminders and positive reinforcement to shift the habits of a lifetime, even if that lifetime has only been six years long! Because of this, I have included a number of child-focused activities and resources to reinforce the messages discussed in the book. The activities are designed to cultivate respect, helpfulness and environmental awareness; they are also good fun.

Children might wish to cut out the *Puppets To Play With* and stick them on craft sticks. They can then use them in their general play, or create productions to show the family about respecting themselves, each other, and the Earth we all share.

They may also enjoy playing *Can you Save Messy?* Each child chooses a name tag and glues it onto a clothes peg. The pegs are then placed in the 'Ready' position on the *Make Your Choice!* Chart which is placed on the wall. Pegs are moved up one position for good decisions and down one position for poor choices. They can only move up or down one position at a time. Choices do not need to be confined to environmental decisions. The game can be used to encourage positive decision making in any facet of life.

At the end of the day, players receive the points next to their peg's position on the chart. For example, if they finish the day on 'Great Choices' they are awarded 2 points. They can then move forward 2 positions on the *Can you Save Messy? Game Board*.

At various points along the Game Board, they are invited to 'Pick a reward card'. They can choose from the reward cards provided or create their own, in line with their preferences and your family values. At the end of the game they receive their *Mega Reward Card. Mega Rewards* involve quality time with their primary caregiver as the 'only child'. This type of 'just me' time is incredibly valuable to a child. Certificates have been included to reward effort. This game is not just about reinforcing positive actions; it is also an opportunity to create irreplaceable childhood memories while you have the chance.

Discussion Time

Key Lesson: Cause and Effect

One of the limitations faced by young children is an incomplete understanding of the process of cause and effect. They simply have not had enough time on the planet to amass the experience required know the difference between a good choice and a bad choice. Therefore, you may wish to help them distinguish between 'A' choices, which produce positive results, and 'B' choices, which produce sub-optimal results. The consequences of our actions may not be immediate and can project many years into the future, but they are inescapable.

You can help your children begin to learn to identify 'A' and 'B' choices by naming them. For example, if you see one of your children drop rubbish on the ground you may like to state, "That's a 'B' choice." You can also add the phrase, "What if everyone did that?" to promote the understanding that we all share the environment; therefore, we all have a responsibility to look after it.

Your family may enjoy using the puppets (included) to create role plays about actions and their inevitable consequences. You can follow the suggestions below, or create your own puppets and stories to share with the family.

- It is lunchtime at school and you are playing with your friends. They start dropping their rubbish all over the ground, instead of using the bin. What do you do?

- You join a bush care project and plant trees on an old mine site. As you clean up the area, and plant trees and shrubs, the animals return. It becomes a place of peace and beauty that everyone can enjoy.

- You go to the beach for a picnic and leave your plastic and rubbish all over the sand. The tide comes up and washes the plastic into the sea. What happens next?

These role plays do not need to be limited to environmental issues. Puppets can be a relaxed, indirect way of prompting discussions on any aspect of your child's life that they may be finding problematic. For example, being teased or left out at school, missing out on a place on a sports team or getting a bad mark in a test.

"Of all the paths you make in life,
make sure a few of them are dirt."

John Muir.

Puppets to Play With!

"Only after the last tree has been cut down,
the last river poisoned and the last fish caught,
will we realise we cannot eat money."

Cree Indian Proverb.

"We could never have loved the earth so well
if we had had no childhood in it."

George Eliot.

My Treasure Bag 1

Find the following items and place them in your treasure bag. Show your parents what you've found!

- ☑ A magic pebble or stone.
- ◯ A fairy's wand.
- ◯ A mermaid's necklace.
- ◯ A unicorn's horn.
- ◯ A frog's crown.
- ◯ A pirate's ship.
- ◯ A magician's cape.
- ◯ A treasure chest.
- ◯ Treasure to put in your treasure chest.
- ◯ Something you think is beautiful.
- ◯ Something you think is special.

"The mountains are calling and I must go."

John Muir.

My Treasure Bag 2

There are 10 items hidden in the Word Find below. Can you find all 10 items in the Word Find and then find them in the garden as well? Show your parents what you have found!

1.

2.

3.

F	A	E	L	N	E	E	R	G	F
N	A	K	D	O	P	D	E	E	S
U	H	B	H	G	R	A	S	S	T
T	K	A	R	S	E	F	W	A	I
F	T	G	I	E	H	R	T	L	C
K	H	E	S	O	T	W	O	E	K
B	E	W	B	R	A	Y	G	O	G
L	D	E	F	T	E	F	K	P	R
K	A	Q	R	I	F	W	C	L	E
R	R	O	C	L	R	R	O	H	R
A	F	W	F	O	B	K	R	L	R
B	A	W	R	E	D	L	E	A	F

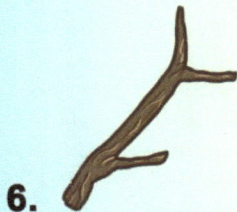

4.

5.

6.

7.

8.

9.

10.

"Do what you can, with what you have, where you are."

Theodore Roosevelt.

Select your peg name tag

Genie

"Away, away from men and towns,
To the wild wood and the downs,
To the silent wilderness,
Where the soul need not repress its music."

Percy Bysshe Shelley.

"The greatest gift of the garden
is the restoration of the five senses."

Hanna Rion.

Pick a reward card!

Pick your MEGA reward card!

Pick a reward card!

Pick a reward card!

Can You Save Messy? GameBoard

Start

1 2 3 4 5 6 7 8 9 10 11 12 13 14 15 16 17 18 19 20 21 22 23 24

"I took a walk in the woods
and came out taller than the trees."

Henry David Thoreau.

Genie

Reward Card

Amber

Reward Card

Max

Reward Card

Tony

Reward Card

Billy

Reward Card

The children of Messy

Reward Card

Leonie

Reward Card

Sue

Reward Card

Puss

Reward Card

Barkley

Reward Card

Messy

Reward Card

Earth

Reward Card

Cut Here !   Cut Here !

My reward is
Stay up 10 minutes later

My reward is
Star gazing before bed tonight

My reward is
One game of my choice with my family

My reward is
Picnic dinner tonight

My reward is
No chores today

My reward is
10 minutes extra to play outside

My reward is
Milkshake after school

My reward is
Teddy bear safari hunt

My reward is
_____

My reward is
_____

My reward is
_____

My reward is
_____

Cut Here !   Cut Here !

Mega Reward Card
Mega Reward Card
Mega Reward Card
Mega Reward Card
Mega Reward Card
Mega Reward Card
Mega Reward Card
Mega Reward Card
Mega Reward Card
Mega Reward Card
Mega Reward Card
Mega Reward Card

Cut Here !   Cut Here !

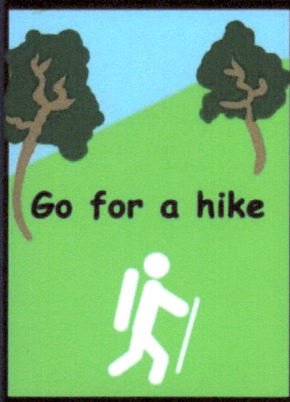

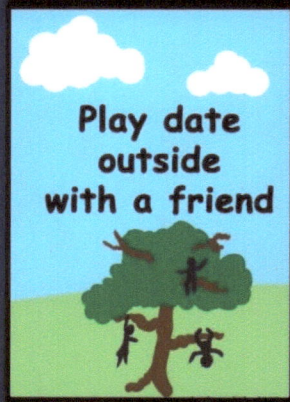

Go for a hike

Play date outside with a friend

PICNIC!

MOVIE night!

Family camping trip

SLEEPOVER!

Visit the playground

Sports day with my family

My Reward is

_____

My Reward is

_____

My Reward is

_____

My Reward is

_____

CONGRATULATIONS

Awarded to

_____

For

_____

"We never know the worth of water till the well is dry."

Thomas Fuller.

CONGRATULATIONS

Awarded to

_____

For

_____

"I don't want to protect the environment.
I want to create a world where the environment
doesn't need protecting."

Unknown.

A Questing Game

If you have limited access to outdoor areas you can use the following *Sleeping Story* and *Questing Game* to generate feelings of connection and tranquility in your child's mind and body. It will also help get them to bed on time!

Slowly, read the script below. Pause at the appropriate places to give them time to imagine the scenes you are describing, and to carry out the instructions.

If you wish, leave a coloured questing card (included) next to their bed, for them to discover in the morning. As children complete each task they can add one colour to their *Kingdom of Nattyboo Game Board*. Blank *Questing Cards* have been included so that you can create personalised tasks that are aligned with the individual needs of your child. When all the colours have been returned to their game board, the location of *The Seeds of Happiness* will be revealed, and children can select their favourite reward card (included).

A Sleeping Story

The script

(Read it slowly. Pause at the appropriate places to give children time to imagine the scenes you are describing, and to carry out the instructions.)

Lie down on your bed, and get into a comfortable position.

Allow your eyes to close gently.

If you don't feel like closing your eyes yet, that's okay, just softly look down.

Take a few slow breaths in and deep breaths out.

You might like to imagine that you're lying on a picnic rug in a clearing in a forest, on a warm sunny afternoon.

Let yourself sink into the rug, on the soft, warm ground as the afternoon sun shines down on you.

You can feel the warm air on your skin.

You can smell the grass, the trees and the flowers all around you as you slowly breathe in and breathe out.

Put your hands on your tummy, and notice how it rises and falls with each breath.

You feel very safe, warm and happy.

Let the warmth of the sun relax your face, neck, shoulders, arms, hands and fingers.

(Leave a small gap between each body part, allowing time for the children to focus on, and then consciously relax, that part of their body).

The sun's rays soak into all the muscles of your chest, tummy, bottom, legs, feet and toes.

You may start to feel very, very heavy.

As you lie there on your soft, warm picnic rug, feeling the afternoon sunshine on your skin, you notice a strange noise coming from your picnic basket.

Rattle, rattle, rattle, rattle.

The noise seems to be getting louder.

RATTLE, RATTLE, RATTLE, RATTLE.

You sit up and open the lid. . . crrreeak.

As you do, you notice the smell of all the delicious food inside. What did you pack for your lunch?

> Steamed vegetables and rice?
>
> A healthy salad or a sandwich?
>
> Or did you pack all of your favourite treats and snacks?

Take a moment now to imagine what you packed in your lunch basket.

Notice how your lunch looks, how it smells and even how it tastes!

Notice what your body does when you do this.

Inside, sitting amongst all your delicious food, is a very large egg. It takes up most of the space in the picnic basket.

What does your egg look like?

Is it gold or silver, rainbow coloured or blue? Is it rough or smooth, shiny or dull?

It's your imagination, and your egg can look however you like.

You reach into the basket, and pick up the egg. It feels heavy, cool and smooth in your hands. Place the egg in your lap, and notice how wonderful it smells.

As you do this, you notice a large crack appears. The shell splits apart and in your lap is a tiny, beautiful, soft, fluffy unicorn.

It looks up at you with its big, baby eyes and says, "Hungry".

You pat its fur and it feels very, very, soft under your hand.

You reach into your picnic basket, and pull out one of your favourite snacks. You give it to the unicorn. Its lips feel soft and wet against your hand as it gobbles up the treat. The little unicorn eats all of the food in your picnic basket and with each mouthful, it grows bigger and bigger and bigger, until the tiny, soft, fluffy unicorn towers over you.

It spreads its enormous wings, and motions for you to jump on its back.

You feel very safe and happy because you know that it's all in your imagination. You can open your eyes any time you like, and you'll be safe and warm in your bed.

You feel completely peaceful and relaxed as you hop on the unicorn's back, and soar off into the still, blue sky. You see your house and your favourite people smiling up at you. You wave and smile back at them as the unicorn flies higher and higher through the soft, misty clouds filled with sunlight. It's so quiet up here. The only sound you can hear is your own breathing, as the air moves in and out of your nostrils.

Listen.

It feels wonderful to be here. You feel completely free and at peace.

Any problems or difficult feelings that you've been having just disappear, as you look down and enjoy your unicorn ride.

You see beautiful forests all around you and huge trees gently swaying in the soft, afternoon breeze. You see enormous, peaceful mountain lakes with the sunlight gently flickering on the water.

In the distance a huge rainbow stretches across the still, blue sky. It has the most brilliant colours you've ever seen. The unicorn flies closer and closer and then, ever so gently, places you on the rainbow. She smiles at you very kindly and tells you that she's been sent from The Kingdom of Nattyboo. She explains that her Kingdom is in great danger as the Seeds of Happiness have fallen from The Tree of Life, and are now lost somewhere in the Kingdom.

Each day the Seeds of Happiness remain missing, more and more magic leaves the kingdom and the children become more and more unhappy. They have forgotten how to play together, laugh and have fun. Only the chosen one – 'The Colourbringer' – has the power to find the lost seeds, return them to The Tree of Life and restore peace and happiness to the kingdom.

The unicorn tells you that of all the children on Earth, you are the chosen one. You are 'The Colourbringer'. You know it's all in your imagination and you can open your eyes any time you like, so you agree to help.

You feel very proud that you will be the one to help find the seeds, and restore peace and happiness to the unicorn's kingdom. Notice how this feels in your body.

It feels so good to help others.

It feels good to be so brave and strong.

You smile. Of all the children on Earth *you* have been chosen.

She tells you that, in order to find the Seeds of Happiness, you must complete six tasks. For the next six nights, some of the fantastic and friendly creatures from her kingdom will visit you while you sleep and leave a coloured Seeds of Happiness Questing Card next to your bed. When you have completed all six quests, the location of the Seeds of Happiness will be revealed.

The unicorn smiles at you, and her horn begins to glow the most brilliant gold. She tells you that the rainbow will take you home. You wave goodbye, and climb onto the rainbow and begin sliding down, down, down. Air rushes past your face. Your whole body is filled with coloured rainbow light - red and orange, yellow and green, blue, indigo and violet. The light pours over you and through you but you're not scared, you're The Colourbringer.

You slide off the end of the beautiful rainbow and into your soft, warm bed. You smile because you know that, in your imagination, you are the Colourbringer. You are happy, brave and strong, and you can return to those feelings any time you like. No matter what kind of day you've had at school or at home, those feelings are always inside you.

You know that you must have a good sleep because in the morning, your first Seeds of Happiness Questing Card will be waiting for you. So, snuggle down into your bed and allow yourself to drift off to sleep.

The Seeds of Happiness

1. **Health** – In this lifetime, you are only going to get one one body, so look after it.

2. **Respect** – Self-respect and respect for others. Contemplate how precious life is and how incredible it is that any of us exist at all. Life is finite, don't waste it.

3. **Gratitude** – If you are reading this book your family is probably within the top three per cent of the wealthiest people on Earth. If you have a healthy body and mind as well, you are likely to be in the luckiest one per cent of the world's population. This makes you very fortunate indeed. However, unrecognised good fortune can result in a sense of entitlement and an inability to appreciate a life of privilege due to a limited perspective. It can be of great benefit to focus on what is right in our lives before we focus on what is wrong. When we do this, our problems can seem much smaller and a deep sense of gratitude for our good fortune can arise.

4. **Kindness** – Acts of kindness create wonderful feelings in our minds and bodies. Be kind to yourself and those around you. Perform spontaneous acts of kindness and notice the sense of joy and peace that this brings.

5. **Connection** – Children (and most adults) crave a sense of belonging, love and acceptance. Help children to understand that we all share the Earth and depend on each other for our happiness and survival. When we separate ourselves from the environment and each other, we can experience a deep disconnect and dissatisfaction with life.

6. **Curiosity** – Be curious about life and the environment and broaden your perspective. When we do this, we can understand ourselves and the world around us better.   This improves the quality of all of our relationships.

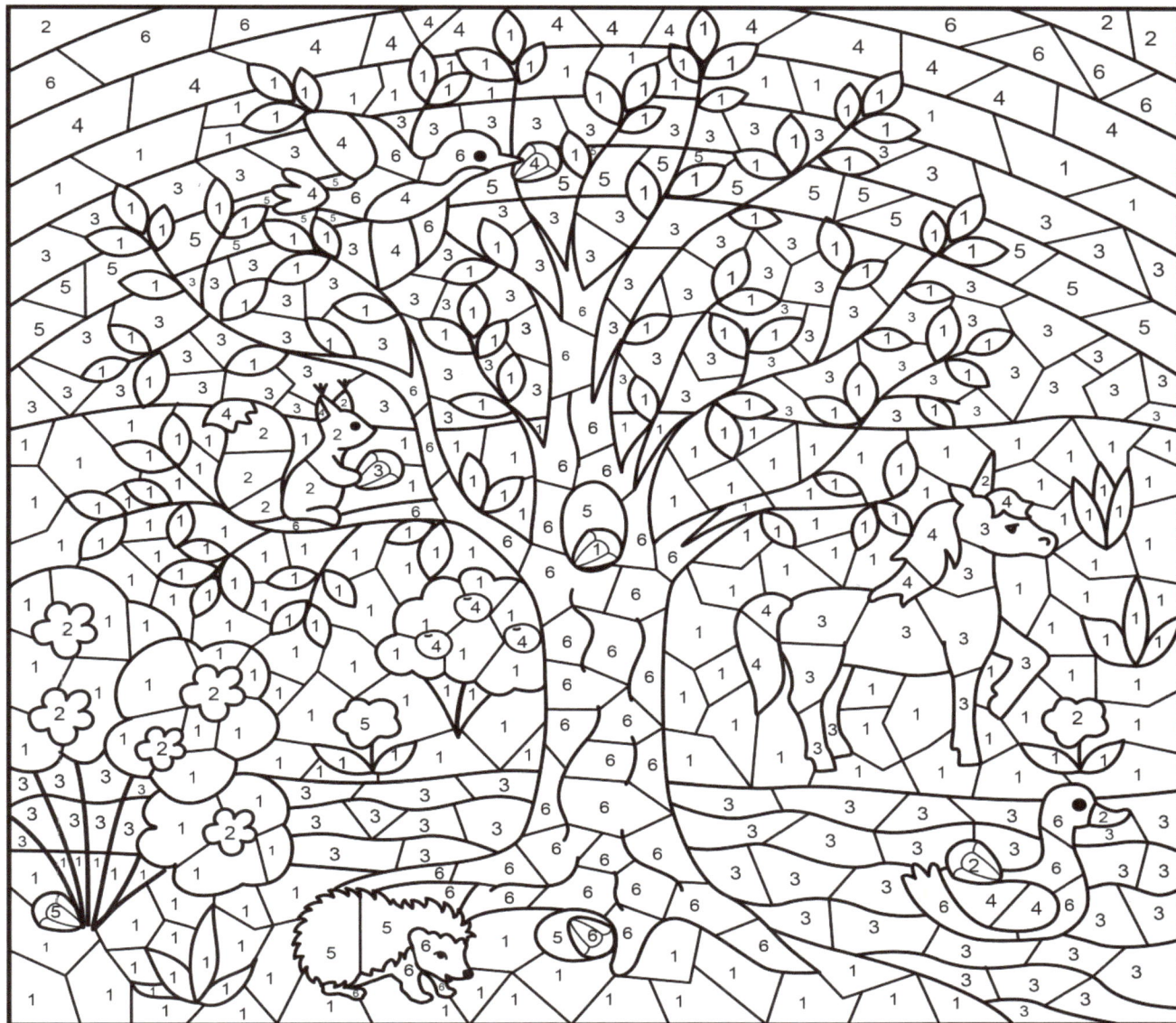

The Kingdom of NattyBoo Game Board

The Seeds of Happiness

As children complete each colour coded quest they add one colour to their Kingdom of Nattyboo Game Board. When all the colours have been returned, the location of The Seeds of Happiness will be revealed and players can select a reward card (included).

"The world of reality has its limits;
the world of imagination is boundless."

Jean-Jacques Rousseau.

Health

Go for a walk in nature.

Take a picnic and play amongst the trees.

Notice the sounds, the smells, and the colours all around you.

Notice how this makes you feel.

Respect

Make 2 decisions today that will make you feel very proud. You might recycle some rubbish, include a child who is sitting alone in your play or offer to help your parents with a job.

Discuss your decisions with your family at dinner.

Notice how good you feel about yourself when you make 'A' choices.

Gratitude

Create a Thankful Jar by upcycling and decorating an old milk carton or jar.

Encourage your family to fill the jar with notes or drawings about the things they are most grateful for. If you can't find a jar, just use a recycled envelope.

At dinner time, discuss the contents of the jar or envelope.

Notice how this makes you feel.

Kindness

Perform three random acts of kindness today. One for yourself, one for someone you know and one for a child you don't know.

They don't need to be big things. You might just share one of your brightest smiles as you walk past another child in the playground.

Notice how you feel when you do this.

Notice their reaction.

Connection

Start a garden from fruit and vegetable scraps. Collect carrot tops, potato pieces, cantaloupe, watermelon, pumpkin or tomato seeds and plant them in a pot containing good quality soil.

Place them in a well-lit place and lightly water them every day.

Watch the vegetables start to grow!

Notice how you feel when you do this.

Curiosity

Pretend you are an alien who is visiting Planet Earth for just one day. Your planet is made of gas, so you find animals, plants and other humans very interesting. Notice how things work, how they feel, smell, look, sound and taste. Keep a holiday diary, so that when you return home you can describe Earth to your alien friends.

Read your *Alien Diary* to your parents at bedtime.

Cut Here !

Cut Here !

Cut Here !

Cut Here !

Cut Here !

Cut Here !

The Bounce Back Series 1

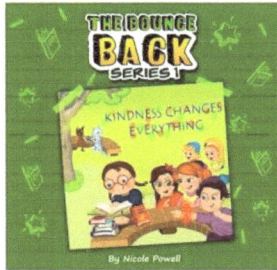

Kindness Changes Everything is the first book in *The Bounce Back Series.* It addresses the serious issue of schoolyard bullying from the perspective of both the victim and the perpetrator. It equips children with the strategies they need to overcome adversity and be resilient when facing such challenges. This provides the most valuable rewards of all: self-respect, respect for others and the opportunity to create enduring friendships.

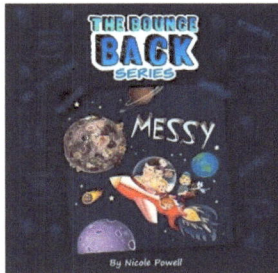

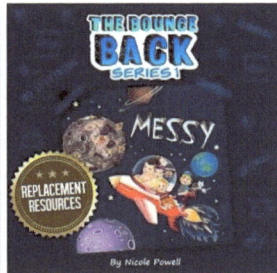

If you enjoyed the resources in *Messy,* but have used them all up, replacement resources are available.

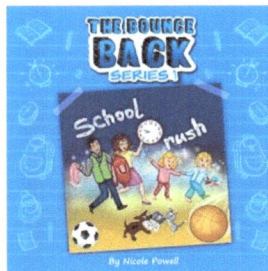

School Rush is the third book in *The Bounce Back Series.* It is designed to help children begin working with their emotions in a positive and healthy way. Instead of school mornings being filled with chaos, frustration and tension, they can be transformed into a time of connection, fun and laughter as you all work together to leave the house on time.

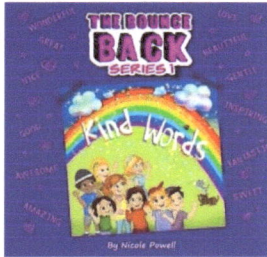

Kind Words is the fourth book in *The Bounce Back Series*. It equips children with the skills they need to resolve conflicts in a calm and assertive manner. Children learn to be gentle with themselves and each other, and as a result, enjoy an improved relationship with themselves and those around them.

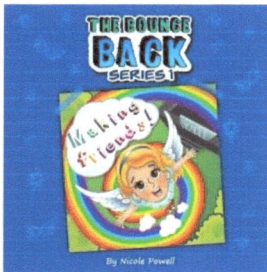

Making Friends is the fifth book in *The Bounce Back Series*. It is designed to help children who find themselves alone in the schoolyard at play. The majority of children will experience this at some point in their school lives. Whatever the cause, this type of social isolation can be extremely distressing to a child (and their parents!) *Making Friends* equips children will the strategies they need to understand their emotions, overcome adversity and be resilient when facing these challenges.

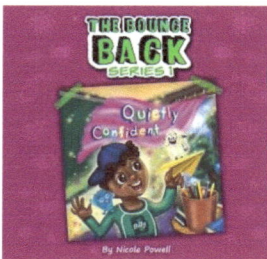

Quietly Confident is the sixth book in *The Bounce Back Series*. It addresses the emotion of Fear which unconsciously underpins many of our choices in life. Billy is desperately afraid of public speaking and it's his turn to deliver a presentation to the class. With the help of Max and the Genie, Billy learns to face his fears. By encouraging children to understand their emotions and take responsibility for themselves and their choices, they enjoy an increased sense of ease with themselves and those around them.

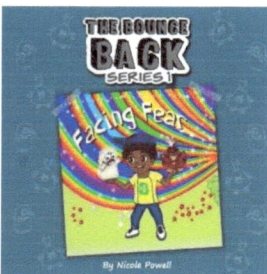

Facing Fear is the seventh book in *The Bounce Back Series*. It helps children to understand that anger is often used to mask the more difficult emotions of fear, emotional hurt, guilt or shame. When children learn to understand their emotions, and face them directly, anger had no reason to arise.

Other books you might enjoy

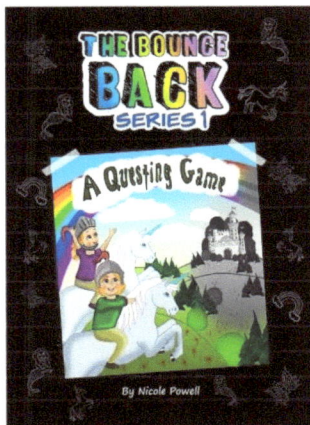

A Questing Game engages children's imaginations as they embark on an adventure that can only begin when they are tucked up in bed at night or calmly resting.

The game encourages children to relax, develops their imagination and cultivates desirable personality traits such as kindness, helpfulness, generosity and compassion. It also encourages a positive internal dialogue which enhances self-esteem and inter-personal relationships.

This game is for anyone who has trouble getting their children to bed at night.

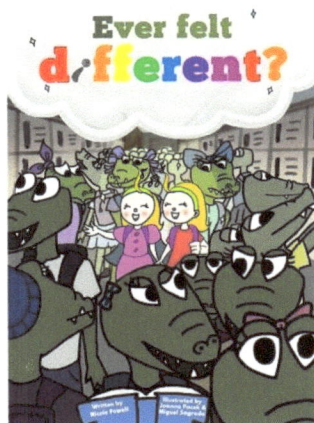

Ever Felt Different? is for anyone who has ever felt different.

Two little girls, delivered to the wrong families at birth by a disorientated stork, have nothing in common with the other children in their neighbourhood.

They don't look the same, behave the same, or like any of the same things.

Although the girls are teased and left out by some of the other children, their mother's love and encouragement helps them to believe in themselves and follow their dreams. They learn to like and accept themselves just as they are and realise that their uniqueness is one of their greatest strengths. In fact, it is only **because** they are different that they soar to great heights.

www.ingramcontent.com/pod-product-compliance
Lightning Source LLC
Chambersburg PA
CBHW060811090426
42737CB00002B/36